Certain Women

LINDA K. BURTON

DESERET
BOOK

Salt Lake City, Utah

Book design © Deseret Book Company
Art direction by Richard Erickson. Design by Sheryl Dickert Smith

Visit us at DeseretBook.com

Library of Congress Cataloging-in-Publication Data
Names: Burton, Linda K., 1952– author.
Title: Certain women / Linda K. Burton.
Description: Salt Lake City, Utah : Deseret Book, [2018] | Includes bibliographical references.
Identifiers: LCCN 2017050691 | ISBN 9781629724379 (hardbound : alk. paper)
Subjects: LCSH: Mormon women—Religious life. | Women—Religious aspects—The Church of Jesus Christ of Latter-day Saints. | The Church of Jesus Christ of Latter-day Saints—Doctrines. | Mormon Church—Doctrines.
Classification: LCC BX8643.W66 B87 2018 | DDC 289.3/32082—dc23
LC record available at https://lccn.loc.gov/2017050691

Printed in China
RR Donnelley, Shenzhen, China

10 9 8 7 6 5 4 3 2 1

CONTENTS

Certain Women Remembered

Whether I travel locally or throughout the world, it is not unusual for someone to ask,

"DO YOU REMEMBER ME?"

Because I am painfully imperfect, I must admit
I often can't remember names.

However,

I DO REMEMBER THE VERY REAL LOVE HEAVENLY
FATHER HAS ALLOWED ME TO FEEL AS I MEET HIS
PRECIOUS DAUGHTERS AND SONS.

Once I had the opportunity to visit some beloved women who are in prison. As we said our heartfelt goodbyes, one darling woman pleaded,

"SISTER BURTON,

please don't forget us."

I hope she and others who want to be remembered will feel so as we reflect on certain women loved by Heavenly Father.

Certain Women in the Savior's Day:

CENTERED IN THE SAVIOR

JESUS CHRIST

Our sisters across the ages have demonstrated the faithful pattern of discipleship that we too strive for.

"The New Testament includes accounts of [certain] women, named and unnamed, who exercised faith in Jesus Christ [and in His Atonement], learned and lived His teachings, and testified of His ministry, miracles, and majesty. These women became exemplary disciples and important witnesses in the work of salvation."[1]

Consider these accounts in the book of Luke.

First, during the Savior's ministry:

"And it came to pass . . . that [Jesus] went throughout every city and village, preaching and shewing the glad tidings of the kingdom of God: and the twelve were with him,

"AND CERTAIN WOMEN, . . .

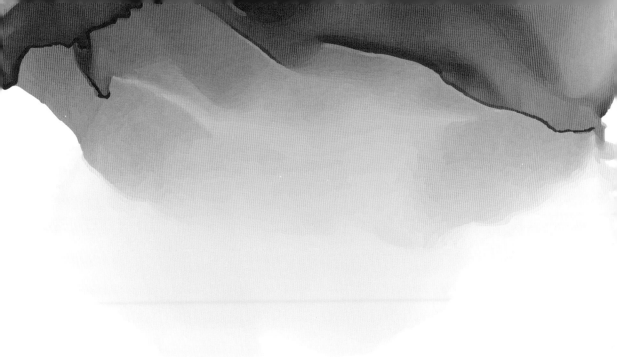

MARY CALLED MAGDALENE, . . .

and JOANNA . . . ,

and SUSANNA,

and many others, which ministered unto him."[2]

Next, following His Resurrection:

"AND CERTAIN WOMEN . . .

which were early at the sepulchre;

". . . When they found not his body, they came, saying, that they had . . . seen a vision of angels, which said that he was alive."[3]

I have read and passed over the seemingly unremarkable expression "certain women" numerous times before, but recently as I pondered more carefully, those words seemed to jump off the page. Consider these synonyms of one meaning of the word *certain* as connected to faithful, *certain women*:

convinced, positive, confident, firm, definite,

assured,
and dependable.[4]

As I pondered those powerful descriptors, I remembered two of those
New Testament *certain women* who bore positive, confident, firm, assured
testimonies of the Savior. Though they, like us, were imperfect women, their
witness is inspiring.

Remember the unnamed woman at the well who invited others to come and see what she had learned of the Savior? She bore her *certain* witness in the form of a question:

"IS NOT THIS THE CHRIST?"[5]

HER TESTIMONY AND
INVITATION WERE SO
COMPELLING THAT

"MANY . . .
BELIEVED
ON HIM."[6]

Following the death of her brother, Lazarus, Martha, the beloved disciple and friend of the Lord, declared with what must have been great emotion,

"Lord, if thou hadst been here, my brother had not died."

Consider her certainty as she continued,

"*But I know*, that even now, whatsoever thou wilt ask of God, God will give it thee."

She further testified,

"I believe that thou art the Christ, the Son of God, which should come into the world."[7]

We learn from these sisters that

CERTAIN WOMEN

are disciples centered in the Savior Jesus Christ and have hope through the promise of His atoning sacrifice.

Certain Women of the Restoration:

WILLING TO SACRIFICE

Anciently, *certain women* sacrificed as they testified and lived the teachings of Jesus. *Certain women* in the early days of the Restoration did the same.

They were similarly taught by the Prophet Joseph Smith "to be righteous individuals, to become a holy people, and to prepare for temple ordinances and covenants."[8]

Their actions demonstrated their commitment and the certainty of their testimonies. As the Kirtland Temple was being constructed, these *certain women* also served as vital participants in the great work of salvation.

Sarah M. Kimball recorded,

"THE WOMEN WOULD CHURN AND CHEERFULLY SEND THEIR BUTTER TO THE WORKMEN ON THE TEMPLE AND EAT WITHOUT ANY ON THEIR OWN TABLES."[9]

The sisters also saw and met a need to make carpets and draperies for the temple. Polly Angell remembered Joseph Smith saying:

"The sisters are always first and foremost in all good works. Mary [Magdalene] was first at the resurrection; and the sisters now are the first to work on the inside of the temple."[10]

One of the ways those faithful sisters worked inside the temple was through service as ordinance workers. Elizabeth Ann Whitney, one of the thirty-six women called as temple ordinance workers in Nauvoo, recalled,

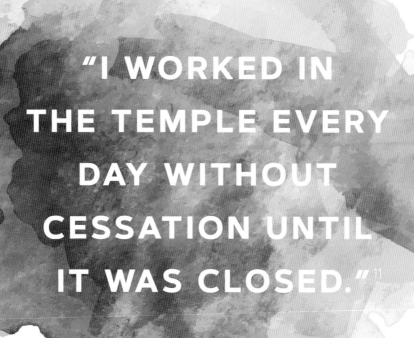

"I WORKED IN THE TEMPLE EVERY DAY WITHOUT CESSATION UNTIL IT WAS CLOSED."[11]

Drusilla Hendricks and her family were among those who, as new converts, suffered during the persecution of the Saints in Clay County, Missouri. Her husband was permanently paralyzed during the Battle of Crooked River. She was left to care for him as well as provide for her family.

"At one particularly distressing time, when the family was out of food, she remembered that a voice told her,

'HOLD ON, FOR THE LORD WILL PROVIDE.'"

When her son was needed to volunteer for the Mormon Battalion, at first Drusilla resisted and wrestled in prayer with Heavenly Father until

"it was as though a voice said to her,

'DO YOU NOT WANT THE HIGHEST GLORY?'

She answered naturally, 'Yes,' and the voice continued,

'HOW DO YOU THINK TO GAIN IT SAVE BY MAKING THE GREATEST SACRIFICES?'"[12]

We learn from these

CERTAIN WOMEN

that covenant-keeping discipleship requires
our willingness to sacrifice.

Certain Women Today:

REMEMBERING AND PREPARING

TO CELEBRATE HIS RETURN

I have mentioned *certain women* in the Savior's day and in the early days of the Restoration of the gospel,

BUT WHAT ABOUT EXAMPLES OF

DISCIPLESHIP AND TESTIMONIES

OF *CERTAIN WOMEN* IN OUR OWN DAY?

On an assignment to Asia, I was once again inspired by the many *certain women* I met. I was particularly impressed with first-generation members in India, Malaysia, and Indonesia who strive to live the gospel culture in their own homes, sometimes at great sacrifice, as gospel living often clashes with family and country cultures.

The multigenerational *certain women* I met in Hong Kong and Taiwan continue to bless the lives of their families, Church members, and communities by remaining centered in the Savior and willingly sacrificing to keep covenants.

Similar

CERTAIN WOMEN

are found throughout
the Church.

A *certain woman* who has blessed my life for decades has battled for the past fifteen years the debilitating, difficult, and progressive disease called inclusion body myositis. Though confined to her wheelchair, Linda strives to be grateful and keeps up her "Can Can List," a running list of twenty-five things she *can* do, such as: I can breathe, I can swallow, I can pray, and I can feel my Savior's love. She bears her Christ-centered *certain* witness almost daily to family and friends.

I can put lipstick on • I CAN HOLD HANDS WITH RICHARD (my hero-hubby)

I CAN KISS RICHARD • I can laugh with Lorna (my twin sis) every

Friday when she comes to do my hair • I CAN ENJOY FAMILY AND FRIENDS

I CAN ATTEND CHURCH, THE TEMPLE, AND SOME EVENTS • I can use

the computer and keyboard • I CAN SEARCH FOR TREASURES OF KNOWLEDGE

I can pray (my heart kneels for my knees) • I CAN FEEL MY SAVIOR'S LOVE

I can choose to be happy & GRATEFUL!

My heart was touched when I heard Jenny's story.

She is a returned missionary whose parents divorced while she was serving her mission. She told how the thought of returning home "scared [her] to death." But at the end of her mission to Italy, as she stopped in the mission home on her way home to the United States, a *certain woman*, the mission president's wife, tenderly ministered to her simply by brushing her hair.

Years later,

another *certain woman*, Terry—a stake Relief Society president and disciple of Jesus Christ—blessed Jenny's life when Jenny was called as a ward Relief Society president. At that time, Jenny was working on her dissertation for her doctoral degree. Not only did Terry serve as a mentor to Jenny as a leader, but she also sat with her for ten hours at the hospital when Jenny received the alarming diagnosis of leukemia. Terry visited the hospital and drove Jenny to appointments. Jenny confessed, "I think I may have thrown up several times in her car."

Despite her illness, Jenny continued to serve valiantly as the ward Relief Society president. Even in her extremity, she made phone calls and sent texts and emails from her bed, and she invited sisters to come see her. She mailed cards and notes to people, loving her sisters from a distance. When her ward requested a photograph of her presidency for their ward history, this is what they got.

Because Jenny is a *certain* woman herself, she invited all to share others' burdens, including her own.

As a *certain woman*, Jenny testified:

"Not only are we here to save others but to save ourselves. And that salvation comes from partnering with Jesus Christ, from understanding His grace and His Atonement and His feelings of love for the women of the Church. That happens through things as simple as brushing someone's hair; sending a note with an inspired, clear, revelatory message of hope and grace; or allowing women to serve us."[13]

Sisters, when we have become distracted, doubtful, discouraged, sinful, sorrowful, or soul-stretched,

may we accept the Lord's invitation to drink of His living water,

AS DID THE *CERTAIN* WOMAN AT THE WELL,
INVITING OTHERS TO DO THE SAME AS WE BEAR
OUR OWN CERTAIN WITNESS:

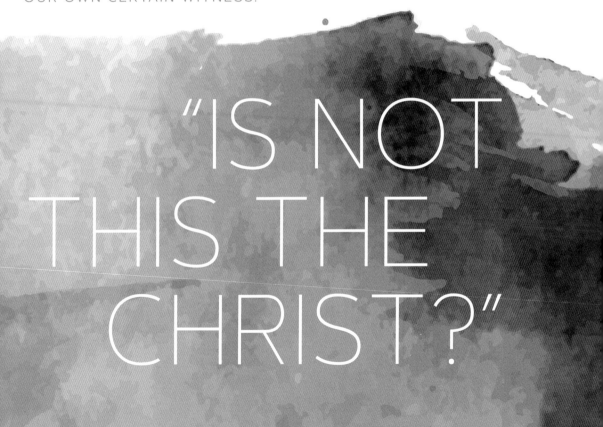

"IS NOT THIS THE CHRIST?"

When life seems unfair, as it must have seemed to Martha at the death of her brother—when we experience the heartaches of loneliness, infertility, loss of loved ones, missed opportunities for marriage and family, broken homes, debilitating depression, physical or mental illness, stifling stress, anxiety, addiction, financial hardship, or a plethora of other possibilities—

may we remember

Martha and declare our similar *certain* witness:

"But I KNOW . . . [and] I BELIEVE that thou art the Christ, the Son of God."[14]

May we remember

the many *certain women* who refused
to abandon our precious Savior
during the excruciating experience He
suffered on the cross and yet hours
later were privileged to be among
the *certain* witnesses of His glorious
Resurrection.

Let us be found staying close to Him in prayer and scripture study.

Let us draw ourselves near to Him by preparing for and partaking of the sacred emblems of His atoning sacrifice weekly during the ordinance of the sacrament and as we keep covenants by serving others in their times of need.

Perhaps then we might be part of the

CERTAIN WOMEN,

DISCIPLES OF JESUS CHRIST, WHO
WILL CELEBRATE HIS GLORIOUS RETURN
WHEN HE COMES AGAIN.

I testify of loving Heavenly Parents; of our Savior, Jesus Christ; and of His infinite Atonement in our behalf. I know the Prophet Joseph Smith was foreordained as the prophet of the Restoration. I know the Book of Mormon is true and was translated by the power of God. We have been blessed with a living prophet in our own day.

OF THESE TRUTHS

I am certain!

Notes

1. *Daughters in My Kingdom: The History and Work of Relief Society* (2011), 3.

2. Luke 8:1–3.

3. Luke 24:22–23.

4. In English the word *certain* has a second meaning of "a selection of" or "a variety of." But it is the meaning of assurance, confidence, and faithfulness that I most wish to emphasize today.

5. John 4:29.

6. John 4:39.

7. John 11:21–22, 27; emphasis added.

8. *Daughters in My Kingdom*, 17.

9. Sarah M. Kimball, in *Daughters in My Kingdom*, 21.

10. Joseph Smith, in *Daughters in My Kingdom*, 22.

11. Elizabeth Ann Whitney, in *Daughters in My Kingdom*, 133.

12. See Jennifer Reeder and Kate Holbrook, eds., *At the Pulpit: 185 Years of Discourses by Latter-day Saint Women* (2017), 51–52.

13. Used with permission of the author, Jennifer Reeder, a specialist in nineteenth-century women's history in the Church History Department.

14. John 11:22, 27.

ABOUT THE AUTHOR

LINDA K. BURTON was born and raised in Salt Lake City, Utah. As a teenager, she spent three years in New Zealand, where her father served as mission president. She attended the University of Utah, studying elementary education. From 2007 to 2010 she served in South Korea with her husband, Craig P. Burton, as he presided over the Korea Seoul West Mission. Sister Burton has served in every auxiliary of the Church and on the Primary and Relief Society general boards. She was called as Relief Society General President in March 2012 and served in that capacity for five years, traveling throughout the world to meet and minister to women. Linda and Craig Burton have six children and 29 grandchildren.

Image Credits

Cover: Image created by Freepik

Pages i, ii, iii, 2, 3, 25: Images created by Freepik
Page v: © Eva Kali/Shutterstock.com
Page vi: © Ajgul/Shutterstock.com
Pages 1, 5, 8, 19, 31: © Karlygash/Shutterstock.com
Pages 1, 5, 19, 31: © Fotosr52/Shutterstock.com
Page 4: © Giftography/Shutterstock.com
Page 6: Image by akdesign/Freepik
Page 6: Painting from the book *This Is Jesus*
   © J. Kirk Richards
Pages 7 and 11: © sibiranna/Shutterstock.com
Page 9: Image by starline/Freepik
Page 11: Image by akdesign/Freepik
Pages 12–13: © Tina Bits/Shutterstock.com
Pages 14 and 20: Image by creative_hat/Freepik
Page 15: Image by creative_hat/Freepik
Page 15: *Women at the Well* © J. Kirk Richards
Page 16: Image by rawstudios/Freepik
Page 16: Image by akdesign/Freepik
Page 16: Painting © J. Kirk Richards
Page 18: © Eva Kali/Shutterstock.com
Pages 20–21: Image by rawstudios/Freepik
Page 20: Kirtland Temple by Shauna Gibby
Pages 22–23: © Eva Kali/Shutterstock
Page 24: Photo of Elizabeth Ann Whitney,
   Public Domain
Page 25: Photo of Drusilla Dorris Hendricks,
   Public Domain

Pages 25–26: © happykanppy/Shutterstock.com
Page 29: © Karlygash/Shutterstock.com
Page 29: © Mehaniq/Shutterstock.com
Page 30: Image by Creative_hat/Freepik
Pages 32–22: © Katsiaryna Chumakova/
   Shutterstock.com
Pages 34–35: © LiskaM/Shutterstock.com
Pages 36–37: © LiskaM/Shutterstock.com
Pages 38–39: Image by rawstudios/Freepik
Pages 40–41: © Eva Kali/Shutterstock.com
Pages 42–43: © Noppanun K/Shutterstock.com
Pages 44–45: © Rudchenko Liliia/Shutterstock.com
Pages 46–47: Image by rawstudios/Freepik
Page 46: *Reflective Waters* © Scott Sumner
Page 49: © Yellow Stocking/Shutterstock.com
Page 50: © NottomanV1/Shutterstock.com
Page 51: © Eva Kali/Shutterstock.com
Page 52: © Melissa King/Shutterstock.com
Page 52: Painting from the book *This Is Jesus*
   © J. Kirk Richards
Page 53: © happykanppy/Shutterstock.com
Pages 54–55: © Eva Kali/Shutterstock.com
Pages 54–55: © Mila_1989/Shutterstock.com
Page 57: Image by harryarts/Freepik

Photographs on pages 34, 35, 38, and 43 are
courtesy of Linda K. Burton.